Written and illustrated by:

ESTEFANIA BRIBIESCA

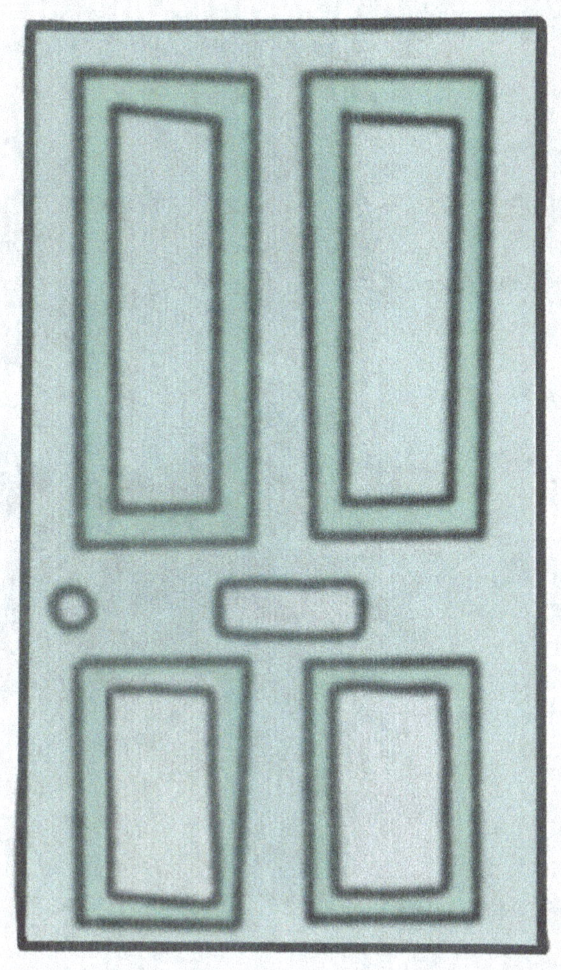

There's a whole world
behind everyone's door.

Juliette

She is sad.
Her parents fight everyday.
She heard they are getting divorced.
It means dad will live in a different house.
She can visit him some days every week.

Charlie

He is mad.
He has a new brother.
Is not that he don't like him,
is just that now he has to share his toys,
and doesn't have his parent's attention the
whole time.

Annie

She is disappointed.
Her best friend suddenly started ignoring her.
She doesn't understand why.
Her BFF didn't give her an explanation.
She just stopped talking to her.

Tommy

He feels anxious.
When mom is not around, he starts
feeling this way.
He can't understand what he's feeling.
He can't even explain it.

Mila

She feels guilty.
She took her mother's makeup to
play, and accidentally broke it.
Now her mom is really mad.

Chris

He is frustrated.
He wants to play the piano,
but his dad makes him practice soccer.
His dad loves football and
he wants Chris to like it too.

Marie

She feels lonely.
Mom and dad work a lot.
She stays in after school activities
until they can pick her up.

Patrick

He is worried.
He heard grandpa is sick.
He can't visit him because the
hospital won't let kids get in.

Rachel

She feels confused.
Dad told her that grandma has died.
She is struggling to understand what does
"grandma is now in the sky" means.

Liam.

He is scared.
Dad comes home late every night.
When he arrives he's usually angry and
start's fighting with mom.

Hazel

She feels overwhelmed.
Her parents and teachers keep telling
her to stay focused and finish her work.
Even though she tries so hard,
she always gets distracted with something.

Jake

He feels lonely.
Mom and dad have been really scared
and anxious during the pandemic.
He's still homeschooling so he hasn't
interacted with kids during all this time.

Violet

She feels shy.
She stutters when she's nervous.
She's been struggling making friends
in her new school because she prefers
to stay in silence.

Lilly

Steve

He feels hurt.
Kids at school laugh at him because
he comes from another country and they
say he speaks a "funny" language.

She feels anxious.
Whenever mom and dad have to go
somewhere else, she starts feeling
this way, and can't stop thinking in
terrible things that could happen to them.

Henry

He feels ashamed.
Yesterday he had an accident in
school (he peed his pants).
Now he can't stop thinking
this could happen again.

Sheila

She feels upset.
Mom won't let her go to her
cousins house this weekend.
No explanation, no reason.
She just said NO.

Paul

He feels jealous.
His dad spends a lot of time
with his cousin because they both
love playing basketball.
He wants his dad to play chess with
him, but he thinks that's boring.

Emily

She feels guilty.
Her goldfish passed away.
She can't stop thinking that she
failed and didn't take enough care for it.

Jack

He feels sad.
He has diabetes, so his diet
is extremely important.
He can't just eat whatever and
whenever he wants to like other kids.

We are all navigating
life's challenges.

Some things feel
new or uncomfortable.

Others feel
unfair or wrong.

Emotions can be
overwhelming.

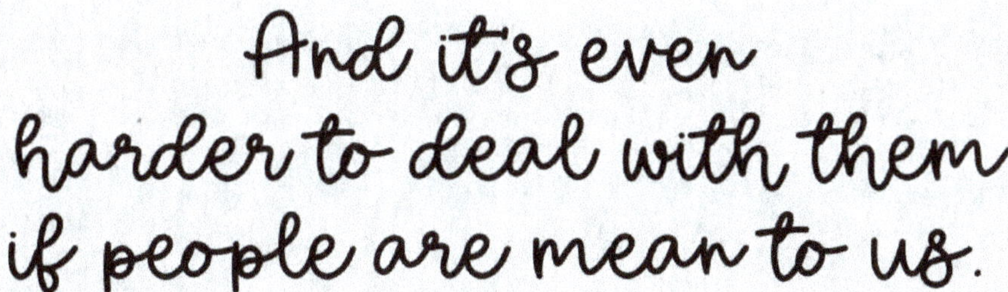
And it's even
harder to deal with them
if people are mean to us.

So be kind to other's.

Don't judge.

Put yourself in
other's shoes.

Demonstrate that
you care.

Ask how you can help.

And if there's
nothing you can do...

You can always give
others one of
your smiles.

Let's build a
community that cares
about each other.

Understanding we are
all struggling with something,
may help us all
be more careful with what
WE THINK, WE SAY, AND WE DO.